# Unique Soul

# Weird World

## By Ron Berman

Scobre Press Corporation
2255 Calle Clara
La Jolla, CA 92037

Scobre Press books may be purchased for
educational, business or sales promotional use.
First Scobre edition published 2007.

Edited by Ramey Temple
Content Editing & Research by Amy Bruinooge
Cover Art & Layout by Michael Lynch
Interns: Julie Sparkuhl & Katherine Shafer

ISBN # 1-933423-87-0

**HOME RUN EDITION**

This story is based on the life of Darren Schaeffer, although some
names, quotes, and details of events have been altered.

We'd like to extend a special thank
you to Darren Schaeffer, AKA Jerry,
for taking many of the awesome
photos that appear in this book.

Thanks Jerry!

*In loving memory of Amy Kritzberger*

# A Letter From Jerry

Hey! I'd like to take this opportunity to introduce myself. My name is Darren . . . Darren Craig Schaeffer, to be exact. But most people call me Jerry, Jairy, Jear Bea, or Jerry Hsu. I'm a senior in high school—actually, I just graduated. I'm on my way to Minnesota State University Moorhead. Soon I'll be a full-time college student.

If people ask me to describe who I am, I simply tell them that I'm *me*. I have many hobbies, including skateboarding, snowboarding, kiteboarding, and longboarding. I'm a musician, a student, and a vegetarian. Some people also say that I'm an artist and a writer.

Many people consider me to be different. They think that I have a unique view of the world. I don't really see it that way. But I do know that I'm definitely not like the average person. I don't want to just *be* different—I want to *make* a difference.

My goal in life is to have fun and make decisions according to what *I* believe. I feel that everyone has a choice about who they want to be. Before people make that decision, they should hear both sides of the story. I'm not here to tell you who to be, just to give you another side of the story.

My personal view is that there's not just

one correct opinion. I live my own life, and I do what's right for me. I try not to force my views on anybody. I am absolutely, positively, not down with small-minded people, pop culture, non-organic food, or anyone who hurts animals. If you have a different point of view, we can agree to disagree.

As you read, I hope you draw your own conclusions about me and about the world. You should understand everything in your own way. Our brains are like our fingerprints—totally our own. We shouldn't be controlled or told how to think by rock stars, movie stars, or politicians. Don't buy into everything you watch on TV, or what you read in the papers. Everybody tells you something for a reason. Be open-minded, but also question everything—even this book.

So anyway, this is my journey, and it belongs to nobody but me.

# Chapter One

## Bury Your Head

*The Wright Brothers: Flyers or Liars*? That was the famous headline on the front page of the *International Herald Tribune*. The date was January 11, 1906. This was three years after the Wright brothers flew an airplane for the first time.

Now, for just a moment, pretend that you are living during this time period. Teddy Roosevelt is the president of the United States. Transportation means a horse and carriage, not a car. Forget MP3 players or even CDs— record players are not even available yet. Imagine your reaction to the news that the Wright brothers have built a machine that allows people to fly!

There were no television cameras in 1903 to show the first flight. So people weren't sure whether or not to believe it. They may have thought that the Wright brothers were dishonest or insane. They probably read many stories with headlines like the one in the *International Herald Tribune*.

Wilbur and Orville Wright refused to give up on their dream, even though they were criticized. It took a lot of guts for them to go for it. The Wright brothers were the big winners in the end, when people saw that their flying machine worked. They became legends. Today, thousands of people board airplanes every day of the year. If not for unique souls like the Wright brothers, this might not have been possible.

There are almost seven billion people living in the world today. Each one of them is completely unique. Sure, a lot of people follow the crowd and do what everybody else is doing. There's nothing wrong with that. However, there are many people who *don't* follow. They see things from a different point of view and aren't afraid to do their own thing. People like that make the world rich, interesting—and, quite honestly, a little bit weird. Their souls flow with ideas never before seen or heard. These creators give us music, new inventions, beautiful art, and huge skyscrapers. Like the Wright brothers, they can also give us something completely new, such as the gift of flight.

Thousands of unique souls are living among us in this weird world. Darren "Jerry" Schaeffer is one of them. You'll find people like Jerry everywhere—in big cities and small towns, and in every corner of the globe. They are young and old, tall and short, rich and poor. They all share a creative spirit that is often questioned by others.

Throughout history, many of these people have been misunderstood. Those who became successful followed their hearts, sometimes even in the face of great criticism. Being unique is about going after your dreams. It's about choosing your own path to travel down, just like the Wright brothers—and just like Jerry.

In 1999, 10-year-old Jerry was preparing to enter middle school in Beulah, North Dakota. He had lived there for three years since moving from Minnesota. A very small city, Beulah has a population of about only 3,000. There's not a whole lot to do there. Jerry could have easily given in to boredom. He could have just settled on a life of TV-watching, snowman-building and video-game playing. Instead, he started skateboarding. He quickly realized that it was going to be a huge part of his life.

"Even at a young age, I got into the skateboarding culture," Jerry remembers. "I realized that being a legit skater wasn't just about the act of skateboarding. I wanted to go deeper. Hopping on your board when you have a little bit of free time doesn't make you a skater. There's so much more. I wanted to bury my head in it, you know? That way, whenever I opened my eyes it would be all around me. So I started bringing my board with me wherever I went, even to school. I hung out with other skaters. I even started to change the way I looked at things."

The experience of being a skateboarder is different for every person. Still, many skaters understand exactly what Jerry is talking about. When you "bury your head in it," skateboarding becomes a way of life, or a *lifestyle*. It affects what you do, how you talk and dress, and how you think about the world.

Part of the "skate cool" lifestyle refers to clothes and other fashion statements. Basically, it's what an individual is all about.

Skater                                    Skater

Jerry likes to wear slim-fit pants that stretch so he can move around more easily. Colorful clothes express his personality. Rain or shine, big shades and hats are part of his wardrobe most days. Shoes are important, too. Jerry likes the pro models from the company *Fallen*.

Some skaters take their style in very different directions. That might mean long hair, spiked hair, or even no hair! You'll see tattoos and piercings, a beanie in the summer, a fake fur hat in the winter. Or, really, any other fashion statement that appeals to them. Sometimes keeping it simple is a statement all by itself—meaning none of the above. The key to being real is being *you*.

Not surprisingly, adults are often the anti-skaters. Young people find it hard to understand *why* adults don't get it—but clearly, most don't. In many cities, lawmakers pass laws that limit the freedom of skateboarders. To them, skaters are troublemaking slackers who should be dealt with harshly.

Maybe some skateboarders *are* slackers, but most are not. Anyway, there are just as many non-skateboarders who fit that description. The two things have nothing to do with one another. There are plenty of awesome skateboarders who are acing tests in school. Not to mention the ones who make loads of cash from successful careers. A lot of people don't take the time to understand skate culture, so they *misunderstand* it. They just assume that skateboarding attracts a bad crowd.

Not all adults are narrow-minded about skating, of course. Many skateboarders from the 1970s and 1980s grew up to be cool adults. Some of them have remained true to the sport. Still, most older people—meaning anyone over thirty—have trouble understanding the appeal of skateboarding. Part of the problem is that skateboarding isn't like baseball or basketball. It isn't focused on winning.

When people think about sports, most of them picture uniforms, rulebooks, teams, and coaches. The focus is usually on wins and losses, points scored, or home runs hit. The thought of a sport that has no real goal seems pointless to some people. Nothing could be further from the truth. When it comes to skateboarding, *having fun* is the point.

Although skateboarding is about pure enjoyment, this doesn't mean that there's anything wrong with competition. Everyone knows that competition is a part of life. We compete in school, in sports, and in our careers. This competitive spirit has made its way into skateboarding. The X Games are proof of that. There are millions of skaters out there skating just for fun. However, there is also a huge community of mainstream skateboarding competition. It's even found its way onto ESPN.

Skateboarding has gone commercial in many ways, but the essence of skate culture has remained underground. When something is "underground," that means it's not accepted by everyone—it's almost the opposite of "mainstream," or "commercial." Skateboarding is a symbol of youth, freedom, and independence. The world would be a boring place if people didn't have a way to express themselves with these kinds of things.

Like almost every other skateboarder in Beulah, Jerry has one main complaint about the city. Beulah is a very flat place! In other words, there aren't many streets that are curving, sloping, or downhill. That's not good news if skateboarding is your thing. You see, Jerry and his friends are "street skaters." They're out on the streets using curbs, benches, stairs, and rails to perform tricks.

In the old days, the place they skated the most was in the parking lot of the grocery store. The best time to skate was at night when all the cars were gone. It was sweet because the parking lot is large and well-lit. The high school was also a good spot for Jerry and his buddies. There are two sets of stairs outside, which were just right for practicing new tricks. But their all-time favorite place was in front of the

Union Bank building.

By the time Jerry and his friends were in seventh grade, they had found other places to skate. However, they still liked kicking it at Union Bank and at the high school. By then, they could do more than just a simple trick like an "Ollie." Jerry had already begun learning more difficult tricks, like Kickflips and Ollie Manuals.

**Jerry, skating around at Beulah High School, practices a new trick.**

Things began to change for Jerry around this time. In the summer after seventh grade, Jerry went to a camp called "701 Board Camp." It was a lot of fun, especially because the camp had an awesome mini-ramp. Jerry had never skated on a ramp before. This was an opportunity for him to learn new tricks. Jerry spent most of his time at camp practicing on the mini-ramp. He and the other campers skated up and down all day long . . . every single day.

Something else happened at camp that was interesting. Jerry, whose real name is Darren Schaeffer, became friends with a kid named Kip. The problem was that Kip, a forgetful kid, couldn't remember his friend's name. As a joke, Kip started calling Darren "Jerry," after a famous skateboarder named Jerry Hsu. Jerry thought this was hilarious, especially when the other kids joined in. The nickname stuck, and now hardly anybody knows that Jerry's real name is Darren!

On the second-to-last day of camp, a mini-ramp contest was held. Jerry had never skated in a competition before. In truth, he didn't really care if he won or lost. He just thought it would be fun to try and pull off some awesome tricks. So, with everybody watching, Jerry went for it. When the contest was over, Jerry had run away with it. He easily won first place and was awarded a brand new skateboard.

Most people, after a successful competition, would get caught up in the thrill of winning. They might feel as if they *had* to continue competing—but not Jerry. "Pretty simple," he says. "I love to skate more than I love to win. Being a pro skater means skating with a bunch of rules. You have to bow down to the sponsors who pay you, which means losing a lot of freedom. Skating for fun means wherever, whenever, and however I say."

When Jerry got home, he had big plans. His experience at camp had given him an idea that was more important than trying to be a pro: Why not try to build a mini-ramp of his own? Forget the sponsors, the skateboard competitions, and the rules. With a mini-ramp in his own backyard, Jerry would be able to skate whenever he wanted.

Jerry was determined to pursue his goal of building a ramp. Having one in his backyard would be the ultimate way to skate in Beulah. He wasn't sure if he would be able to do it, but he was ready to try. As soon as he returned home, he talked to his dad about the idea. Mr. Schaeffer was interested. He was also very supportive and felt that it was a worthwhile project. So Mr. Schaeffer talked to a friend who had experience in construction.

For his part, Jerry borrowed a book from a friend on how to build a skate ramp. The book was a great help. Jerry also did hours of online research. Finally, he was ready.

Luckily, it was still summer, because Jerry had a lot of work ahead of him. He thought he might be able to complete the project in a week or two. He and his dad purchased a bunch of wood and brought it all home. The next morning, Jerry woke up at the crack of dawn and began. It was a little confusing, and things got off to a slow start. But Jerry didn't care. He's the kind of guy who sets his mind to something and then just goes out and does it.

Working nonstop, Jerry ended up finishing far ahead of schedule. With almost no help, he built his mini-ramp in just four days! He named it "El Mini." Over the years, he has redone the surface of El Mini a couple of times so that it remains smooth. That makes it easier to ride. Still, nothing can compare to the day he completed it. When Jerry's friends came over, they were totally stoked—yelling and fighting over who got to try it out first.

The feeling of satisfaction within Jerry was amazing. He spent the rest of the summer skating on that mini-ramp . . . and many summers since then.

**El Mini**

# Chapter Two

## The Mainstream Thing

It's very difficult to describe skateboarders. How can you label them when they are all so different? There are young people like Jerry, who don't care about contests, sponsorship, or being famous. But there are also many skateboarders out there who are more mainstream. They may even dream of going pro one day. "Either way, it's about having fun," Jerry insists. "Yeah, maybe some people have different goals than I do. But hopefully they're still out there for the love of it."

Jerry has a good attitude about this lifestyle. Most kids don't start out trying to become famous or rich. For them, skateboarding is just a fun hobby. In some cases, though, these things eventually do become important to them. As Jerry says, "Skateboarding is whatever you want it to be." The main reason it has become more mainstream is because of its booming popularity. This isn't a bad thing, because it will get more people interested. It will probably mean more skate parks, skate clothing, and skater music.

Superstar skateboarders have definitely added to the popularity of the sport. One name that immediately comes to mind is Tony Hawk. Tony was born in San Diego, California, in 1968. His introduction to skateboarding took place when he was just 9 years old. Tony's progress was quick and impressive. By the age of 12, he was already sponsored. By 14, he was a pro. By the time he was 16, he was regarded as the best skateboarder in the world.

Many people think Tony Hawk led the way in this modern age of skateboarding. This may be true, because Tony has been followed by a wave of new skateboarding stars. One of them is 17-year-old Ryan Sheckler, of San Clemente, California.

Ryan's career has taken off over the past few years. He's won the X Games, Gravity Games, and Van's Triple Crown since turning pro. He's also won a ton of awards. They include being named the 2005 Dew Action Sports Tour "Athlete of the Year." Yes, Ryan Sheckler is as mainstream as it gets. However, he's out there for all the right reasons, just like Jerry. As Ryan says on his website, "Skateboarding is my life. I do it because I love it."

Another skateboarder who feels the same way is Paul Rodriguez, Jr. You might know him as "P-Rod." He's an example of someone who made his own way in life, without any help. It might have been easier for him to go into show business. After all, he's the son of famous comedian Paul Rodriguez. But P-Rod dreamed of becoming a pro skateboarder. He fell in love with skateboarding at the age of 12. With hard work, he made that dream come true.

P-Rod and Ryan Sheckler are no different than Jerry. For all of them, it always seems to come back to the same thing: a true love of the sport. In an interview with *Skateboarder Magazine*, P-Rod said, "I didn't skate to please everyone else. I started skating because I love to skate."

Becoming a professional skateboarder is a difficult goal to achieve. There are millions of kids across the country competing for a handful of spots. Anyone who knows the history of skateboarding understands how hard it is. After all, this was once an underground sport. Sponsorship dollars and advertising deals simply weren't handed out. Only recently has it been geared to a larger audience. This popularity means that big dollars have finally become part of the sport. Still, in terms of money, skateboarding is far behind sports like football, baseball, and basketball.

Money was the *last* thing on anyone's mind back in the early days of skateboarding. The original idea was to copy surfing, but on land. California surfers built homemade skateboards. That way they would have something to do on days when the waves were flat. The sport is said to have started in the 1930s. But some people believe that it existed even before then.

**Grandma's still kickin' it: One of the original skateboard pioneers prepares for the X Games (just kidding!).**

In the beginning, skateboards were basically just pieces of wood set on wheels. It wasn't until the late 1950s that more modern-looking skateboards began to appear. By the 1960s, skateboards were selling very well and the sport was becoming popular. However, skateboards back then had inexpensive clay wheels. It was difficult to turn without falling. Compared with the skateboards of today, it's hard to imagine how people rode those things.

Through the years, skateboarding has gone through many ups and downs. The first skateboard competition took place in Hermosa Beach, California, back in 1963. It was an exciting time for this up-and-coming sport. Unfortunately, just a couple of years later, interest in skateboarding fell off. One of the reasons for this change in popularity was that skateboarding was banned in some cities. Numerous injuries, and even some deaths, had occurred as a result of skateboarding accidents.

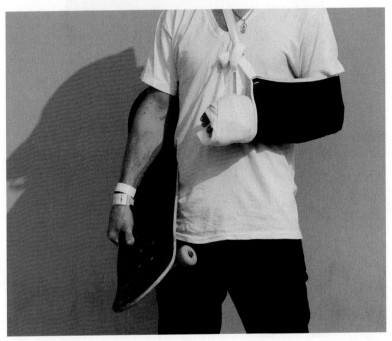

It may have been the poor equipment. Or maybe it was the inexperience of the young people who were taking up this new sport. In any case, for many years skateboarding was viewed negatively. This caused the sport to go underground.

Luckily, by the 1970s, things began to pick up again. The equipment improved and so did the popularity of skateboarding. The invention of the urethane wheel in 1972 led to the creation of new boards. These new boards were capable of handling the amazing tricks we've all become used to. Around the same time, skate parks began to pop up everywhere. These parks were great places for skateboarders to show off their skills. These days, skate parks are huge, modern, and in some cases open 24 hours a day.

Skateboarding's comeback in the 1970s led to new tricks. Probably the most famous of these was the Ollie. It was invented in 1978 by a skateboarder named Alan Gelfand. This was an exciting period of time for skateboarding. The skaters of that era were even shown in a 2005 movie, *Lords of Dogtown*.

There was yet another quiet period in the skateboarding world during the early 1990s. Then, suddenly, a whole new wave of popularity took hold. Skateboarding had become part of the growing interest in extreme sports. Every year, these sports pick up more and more momentum. There are major extreme sports competitions. The X Games, Gravity Games, Van's Triple Crown, and the Dew Action Sports Tour are some of them.

Things have changed dramatically since the 1960s and 1970s. Back then, it was basic equipment and one-dimensional tricks. A simple Ollie was cool. Who would have thought of the amazing things skateboarders would be doing 30 years later? Tricks like jumping over the Great Wall of China on a skateboard sound impossible. But pro skateboarder Danny Way made history by doing just that on July 9, 2005.

That insane feat even impresses Jerry. True, he isn't really a big part of the whole mainstream thing. Still, he's a loyal skateboarder at heart. That's why he's got nothing bad to say about anybody who enjoys some form of skate culture. It's like music. Maybe you're into metal or alternative. There's no reason to look down on someone who's into pop or rap. It's just a matter of personal taste.

Jerry sums it up quite well, saying, "My life means my choice. There is nothing wrong with mainstream skateboarding, TV, or music—but for me, mainstream *anything* seems like a lazy way to entertain myself. I don't automatically like stuff just because it's on the radio or TV. My attitude is: be bold. Find new bands, videos, and other things, 'cause they're definitely out there."

# Chapter Three

## Next to Nothing

The song begins with a bone-crunching guitar intro. Then the drums kick in, followed by the thumping of Jerry's bass. The guys in the band look at each other and smile. Nothing gives them more satisfaction than sounding good. When the lead singer steps up to the mic, everybody gets even more fired up. They are totally in the moment, jamming with intensity (and, of course, loud volume). When they are rocking out, there's no holding back.

At times like these, Jerry's entire house tends to shake. "Yeah, we can definitely get loud down there," he says. "I'm sure there were times when my parents wondered if it was an earthquake." Luckily, Jerry's parents can rest easy. The state of North Dakota has rarely experienced an earthquake.

It's hard to imagine anyone loving music more than Jerry. Just like skateboarding, he brings passion to his music. Being a bass player is all about rhythm, instinct, and a feel for what sounds good. The combination of his bass and the drums forms the backbone of the band.

Lead singers usually get most of the attention, not bass players. That's just fine with Jerry. He's in it for the music. For him, it's about the thrill of creating something original. Jerry also loves seeing the looks on people's faces when his music moves them.

Being in a band gives musicians like Jerry a special feeling. It's hard for him to even put it into words. Having the ability to affect people with your music is a gift. Anyone who has ever picked up an instrument knows that it's not easy. There's also the satisfaction of hearing new music that you have created. Everybody can relate to the thrill of listening to a great song for the first time. It's even cooler to be one of the people who performed the song.

Music is a deep and magical force for people all over the world. It's been that way for as long as mankind has existed. Many experts believe that music dates all the way back to the cavemen! These days, music is part of many of the celebrations we enjoy. It's hard to imagine holidays, weddings, religious ceremonies, and sporting events without music.

Everyone is into music. A lot of older people love classical music, or popular songs from when they were young. Teenagers have always shown an interest in a wide variety of music. If you turn on your radio you'll hear rap, R&B, alternative, metal, country, and contemporary pop. Everybody has their own favorite style.

And then there's Jerry. His passion for music stretches far and wide. The music he likes doesn't fit into any type of top-40 format. His broad taste reflects his unique personality. When Jerry was in eighth grade, his fascination with music became serious. At that time, he had a good friend named Brett Anderson. Brett's older brother exposed Jerry to a whole new world of alternative music.

The turning point for Jerry was when he and Brett stopped listening only to the radio. They started searching the Web, and downloading music from underground bands. In addition, they talked to older kids about the different types of music they were into. It was all about digging up new, *hidden* music. When Jerry and Brett came across good new bands, it was twice as rewarding. "Pop music can be shoved down your throat if you let it," Jerry says. "I look hard to find *my* music. I don't just let it find me."

The two friends discovered that just listening to music wasn't enough. They were driven to make music of their own. Brett was a guitar player and they knew a kid who was a drummer. They had another friend who could sing. All they needed was a bass player. Jerry decided that he was the man for the job. So he bought a bass guitar and learned how to play. It took only a few months for Jerry and Brett to go from fans to members of a band.

Jerry had never taken any music lessons, but he showed talent for the bass. It helped that he was enthusiastic. Jerry practiced all the time, both with the guys and on his own. Next thing they knew, "Next to Nothing" was born. Braden, one of the band members, came up with the name. It's a pretty clever name, especially because of what it means . . . absolutely nothing (actually, *next* to nothing!). It was the perfect name to capture the spirit of this cool new band.

Next to Nothing consisted of eighth and ninth graders. None of them had much experience playing or performing. Still, they ended up doing very well for several years. They even traveled to Bismarck, North Dakota, and recorded a demo at a recording studio. It contained three songs they wrote themselves. People at their school and in Beulah liked the demo. That led to the band's greatest accomplishment: live performances.

Over a period of three years, Next to Nothing did a number of shows in Beulah. They would rent out the rec. center and charge a few bucks at the door. "It wasn't about making money," Jerry explains. "It was about having fun and playing for an audience. We wanted everybody to come and have a great time. We charged just enough to break even."

The formula was a total success. At one of their shows, over 400 people showed up. Remember, Beulah is a very small town, so that's pretty amazing! Another time, the band got a taste of what it must be like for real rock stars. The mother of one of the band members rented a limo for them. They showed up to their gig in superstar style.

It was an exciting time for Next to Nothing. Performing live is a rush, especially when it's in front of friends and classmates. There were many unforgettable moments, including a show they did for charity. During Jerry's freshman year of high school, one of his classmates was diagnosed with cancer. The school decided to hold a charity event to raise money for his treatment. Jerry is still proud that Next to Nothing was one of the performers for that worthy cause.

When Jerry doesn't have a musical instrument in his hand (and isn't skateboarding), he's probably listening to music. How into music is he? Well, Jerry owns over 100 gigs of songs on his computer. That's over 20,000 songs! He normally carries his 80-gig Archos 504 wherever he goes. This device plays music, videos, movies, and displays photos. Jerry prefers the Archos 504 over the iPod. Typical Jerry, always choosing something that's less mainstream.

Jerry indicates on his MySpace page exactly what kinds of music he enjoys. His profile says, "I listen to a wide variety of bands in different styles: hardcore, emo, post-hardcore, indie, metal, and just about anything with a piano." He then lists about 100 of his favorite bands.

Jerry recently made a change as a musician. Already a skilled bass player, he decided he needed a new challenge. He chose to learn guitar. Jerry took to the instrument almost immediately. He now loves playing guitar as much as the bass. Even though he has graduated from high school, this doesn't mean he'll stop playing. He's already formed a new band that will be performing at his college. He'll get to play both bass and guitar, depending on the song.

There's nothing Jerry enjoys more than attending live shows. Among other events, he went to see the indie metalcore band Killswitch Engage last year. He also attended the Grind Your Face Off Fest in Bismarck, which featured more than 20 bands. At that festival, he rocked out to Skarp, Magrudergrind, and Mouth Sewn Shut.

Jerry enjoys these all-day festivals. It's an opportunity to see a lot of different bands. Last year he went to Summer Scene, another festival that featured various bands. He's also looking forward to attending the well-known Warped Tour. It will roll through the neighboring state of Minnesota soon, and he'll be there.

Things are going to get even better when Jerry goes off to college. Being a college student will mean more freedom. Not only that, but older college students will definitely share Jerry's passion for music. Hopefully some of them will share his sense of adventure in finding new bands. "I can't wait," Jerry says.

"I have a feeling I'll be going to shows every single weekend."

# Chapter Four

## Classic Jerry

Jerry stared at the computer screen, looking at a painting of a horse. The computer was playing "Living Each Day Like You're Already Dead." This is a song by the band Atreyu. Jerry sat there staring at the painting for a long time. He does this sometimes. He tunes out the rest of the world and sits at his desk. He thinks about stuff or looks at cool things online.

Connecting to art on a deep level can be a rewarding experience. It isn't something a lot of people do every day. Jerry appreciates art in the same way he appreciates music. Both art and music are ways for a person to be creative. Jerry likes to study art and ask questions: *What was the artist thinking? Why did he pick certain colors? Is that just a horse, or does it mean something different?*

Jerry's been interested in art for a long time. So it makes sense that he would study it on his own. He got into drawing recently, a hobby he really enjoys. One of his friends is studying art in college. This friend has an eye for talent and he likes Jerry's work. So do many other people. All of these positive reactions have given Jerry a boost of confidence. This is important as he continues to explore his artistic side.

It makes sense that Jerry is into skateboarding, music, and art. For a lot of skaters, these hobbies go together. "Skate art" takes on many different forms—clothing, tattoos, paintings, photos, and videos. Mostly, though, the art is all about the skateboard itself.

Through the years, many skateboarders have enjoyed putting stickers on the top side of their boards. The top side of a skateboard is also called a "deck." The stickers represent their favorite bands, movies, or anything else. They are forms of art that reflect the skater's personality. Skaters are unique people. If they all had the exact same decks, it wouldn't be as interesting. Expressing themselves in unusual ways is part of what makes them tick.

Sticker art is just the beginning. Skaters also use pens or paint markers to write on their decks. Some choose inspirational phrases like "Mind over matter." Others write strange statements that seem to make no sense at all. For example: "My brain is made of wood," or "Hungry road eater." Jerry has even seen people carve words into their boards with rocks or scissors.

Many artistic skaters create their own colorful decks. The sky's the limit as far as what they can do. Graffiti, stenciling, painting . . . you name it, and it's probably been done. For his part, Jerry has created some awesome decks.

The song by Atreyu ended and Jerry looked away from the horse. He returned his attention to his calculus book. There was an exam coming up and he wanted to be totally prepared for it.

Jerry knows he can do well in any class he sets his mind to. Still, he's not interested in being a robot. He doesn't want to just memorize information. Jerry wants to know the *how* and *why*. As a confident person, he's not afraid to ask questions and give his opinion. Sometimes his teachers are surprised by this direct approach. But that's classic Jerry. He has his own ideas and insists on doing things his own way.

**Jerry does things his own way. In this photo, he might be heading out to do some skateboarding or snowboarding ... or he may just be going downstairs for dinner!**

Jerry likes to challenge himself and develop his mind by reading a lot. No subject is too difficult for him. He has even read several books on quantum physics. That's not exactly easy reading! Luckily, Jerry also reads stuff normal people can relate to. Stephen

King happens to be one of his favorite authors.

On top of everything else, Jerry is also a talented writer. He approaches a blank page in the same way he begins one of his drawings. His viewpoint is that of a teenager who sees the world in a special way. The stories he creates reflect his life. A lifetime of skateboarding and interesting hobbies affects his writing. Like his art, his writing can't be put in a box. He doesn't go for the predictable. Instead, he goes wherever his imagination takes him—as in the story of *The Angry Doughnut.* If you feel like checking out his story, here you go:

### *The Angry Doughnut*
### By: Darren "Jerry" Schaeffer

**Once upon a time, on an ordinary day, on an ordinary planet comprised of silicon, with an atmosphere largely made up of nitrogen that orbited a normal third generation star, in an ordinary solar system, on the outer edge of an ordinary spiral galaxy, that at its center has a normal black hole, that emits normal radiation (AKA Earth) was a powdered doughnut named Thomas, or Tom-Tom for short.**

**No one knew why he was called Tom-Tom, because Tom-Tom is undoubtedly just as difficult to say as Thomas. Tom-Tom was not your average doughnut. For one thing, he could freely**

34

think, which is pretty extraordinary in itself. He was also incredibly angry. His anger didn't stem from a conventional source–like he had recently lost a loved one or wasn't held as a child. Tom-Tom was angry because the hole at the center of him wasn't round or oval—it was square. On top of that, he had a mad case of ADHD that often made him consume large amounts of cookies at one time.

Sometimes, usually the first, third, and fourth Tuesday of each month, he would go on destructive rampages through France. His hatred of France, which dwelled deep within his layers of dough-nutty goodness, was greater than his hatred towards his abnormally shaped hole. To make things worse, every once in a while, mid-rampage, his ADHD would kick in, and he would forget what he was initially angry about. This would make him even angrier.

As a result of his increased anger, he would breathe out garden gnomes. These gnomes weren't alive, they just made everyone who looked at them extremely angry, and crave cookies. Ever since anyone could remember, Tom-Tom had terrorized this planet of highly evolved apes ... until one day, when a very special hemorrhoid gave an extremely special telephone pole some peculiar magical powers.

This telephone pole, whose name was

Timmy or Tim-Tim for short, was no ordinary telephone pole. He was always happy. One day while Tim-Tim held up a line during a routine call, he developed a massive hemorrhoid. His hemorrhoid developed because he sat too much. What do you expect? He was a telephone pole—sitting was his life!

About a week after he developed his legendary hemorrhoid, he had a super-crazy craving for triple-chocolate double-frosted fudge cookies. All he could think about was triple-chocolate double-frosted fudge cookies. And after about an hour of intense craving, they started to appear out of thin air. At first, Tim-Tim thought he was imagining things. After much mental anguish he came to the conclusion that his hemorrhoid had given him the power to turn flowers into triple-chocolate double-frosted fudge cookies. Now, these cookies were extremely special, because anyone who ate them became unhealthily happy.

One day, while Tom-Tom was in the middle of an ADHD-fueled rampage, he got distracted by what appeared to be a large field of triple-chocolate double-frosted fudge cookies. He went over to investigate, and on the way he noticed a very tall, very elegant, very *French* telephone pole. This made him angry, but his ADHD was so strong that he forgot about the telephone pole. So with the fleeing feeling of anger, and an increasing desire for triple-chocolate double-frosted fudge cookies, he proceeded to the field.

Approximately 28.678 seconds later, he was at the field, stuffing his face with the greatest cookies he had ever tasted. He ate so many cookies that the goodness of them overcame the anger that boiled deep within Tom-Tom, and his square hole transformed into a picture-perfect round doughnut hole. As a result of his new perfect body, he had no reason to be angry, and never terrorized the world again.

So, there you have it. Jerry's one-of-a-kind storytelling!

Writing, just like art and music, is a personal experience. Everyone has his or her own taste and will be affected by Jerry's writing in a different way. This doesn't only apply to Jerry. Creative people have always expressed themselves in their own way. Throughout history, some of them were laughed at or punished for being different.

One example is the legendary Pablo Picasso. He is one of the most famous painters in history. Incredibly, his paintings were not well liked at first. He painted the human body in ways that made people uncomfortable. He might put an eye on a person's hand, or give someone three feet or two heads. In the beginning, his work was totally misunderstood and criticized.

**Because of visionaries like Picasso, a new generation of artists enjoy the freedom to express themselves.**

It would have been easier for Picasso to simply create "normal" art. But that obviously wasn't what he felt in his heart. He continued taking risks and painting in his own style. Now, many years after his death, he is regarded as a genius. Picasso is known as one of the fathers of modern art.

Maybe one day in the future, people will read *The Angry Doughnut* and think that Jerry is a genius.

# Chapter Five

## Snowman

As we've learned, Jerry is involved in many different activities. He's a skateboarder, a musician, an artist, and a writer. He's also into winter sports, which makes sense when you live in Beulah, North Dakota. The average temperature in Beulah during the winter months is a freezing 10 degrees!

Despite its weather, North Dakota is all about the outdoors. This farming state has a population of about half a million people. North Dakotans seem to love doing things outside. There are many state parks, lakes, rivers, and mountain ranges. This means there are excellent places to fish, hike, and explore. However, Jerry isn't into most of these things. He's got a whole different set of interests—which are as unique as he is.

Jerry likes to say that if it has the word "board" in it, he's down for it. "Obviously, skateboarding is number one," he says, "but I also love longboarding and snowboarding." Longboarding is a form of skateboarding. It uses a board that is longer than a normal skateboard. A longboard is built for speed and can be used for downhill racing.

Jerry bought his longboard on the Internet. He and his friend Rocky have taken this sport to the extreme. "Rocky and I have gone longboarding at strange times and in strange places," Jerry explains. "We've done some *insane* stuff!"

Jerry is quick to warn young people about this dangerous sport. It is risky unless you have a great deal of experience with longboarding. A lot of safety equipment is necessary. "If you don't want to get mangled, you need to be prepared with a helmet and all kinds of pads."

Jerry and Rocky have enjoyed many adventures together over the years. They've spent tons of time skateboarding in Beulah. During the winter, they hang out in Bismarck at the indoor skate park. Because of the freezing temperatures in North Dakota, there's no other choice. Skaters appreciate having this indoor skate park.

When winter hits North Dakota, the skateboard season moves indoors. This is Red River, in Fargo, North Dakota.

The city of Bismarck is the capital of North Dakota. It is one of the largest cities in the state. Jerry and Rocky drive from Beulah to Bismarck to skate at the Savvy Skate Shop. One of the nice things about driving in North Dakota is that there's not a lot of traffic. You have to be careful, though, because the state has some pretty out-of-date laws. You probably won't get into trouble, but the laws still exist. For example, in North Dakota, it is illegal to lie down and fall asleep with your shoes on! What genius came up with *that* one?

As Jerry has said, one of the negatives of living in Beulah is that it's really flat. That's another reason why he and Rocky prefer traveling to the hilly streets of Bismarck. They have spent many awesome days there, skating around and just listening to music. Some of the bands Jerry likes to listen to while skateboarding are: The Devil Wears Prada, Job for a Cowboy, and The Audition.

Part of what makes it fun is that the two friends are easygoing. Jerry and Rocky aren't caught up in trying to accomplish anything. "It would take a lot of the fun out of it if we were skating competitively," Jerry explains. "Then, it would be like, 'I *have* to do this trick, or I *have* to beat this time.' As far as we're concerned, we don't *have* to do anything."

Jerry feels the same way about sponsorship. He understands that some skaters set sponsorship as a goal. But it has very little importance to him. In truth, he's never looked at it as something worth the bother. "Yeah, it would be nice to get free stuff, but at what price, you know? I'm out there skating, listening to good music, and learning new tricks—*my way*. That's enough for me."

When Jerry mentions tricks, every skateboarder will probably nod his or her head. They are the very heart of skateboarding. Sure, it's fun to just skate around with your friends. But learning tricks is what it's truly all about. Mastering a trick is a feeling that's hard to describe. Beginning skateboarders start out by learning the Ollie. It's an important step. Almost every other trick involves the Ollie in some way. A skateboarder has to be skilled in doing an Ollie before trying just about anything else.

An Ollie is when you kick down with your back foot at the tail of the board. That sends the board flying upwards. At the same time, you jump in rhythm and try to keep your balance.

Another of the many tricks Jerry has perfected is the Ollie Manual. This is a trick where he performs an Ollie but then ends up on his back wheels. He rides a "wheelie" as long as possible before setting the front wheels down. This trick took Jerry a long time to master. Skateboarding tricks require a good sense of balance. More than anything, though, they take a ton of practice.

Tricks are also a big part of snowboarding, another sport Jerry recently got into. Believe it or not, his favorite spot to snowboard in Beulah is the local golf course! In the winter, nobody can golf because the grass is covered with several feet of snow. The small hills on the golf course are perfect for a snowboarder to do jumps.

Always on the lookout for fun and original hobbies, Jerry has discovered another one. It's called snowkiting. A pretty new sport, snowkiting has only been around for about ten years. It's a cross between skiing, snowboarding, and windsurfing. Snowkiting usually takes place on the snow. A snowkite has a board and a kite, which looks like a parachute. The snowkiter is pulled along the ground and through the air by the kite. The snowkite, like other kites, uses the power of the wind to move.

Snowkiting is taking off because of young people who enjoy trying out new things. In fact, an interesting and educational snowkiting trip was recently made in North Dakota. The leaders of the trip were two snowkiters named Sam Salwei and Jason Magness. They set out on a 370-mile snowkiting trip across the state. The idea was to teach people about this new sport. Another goal of the trip was to draw attention to wind power.

This is more important than it sounds. Wind power could have a huge impact on the environment, pollution, and even the safety of our country. It's possible to use the power of the wind to make energy. Then, the United States would not need as much oil, which causes pollution.

**Generating energy from the wind.**

The United States buys most of its oil from countries in the Middle East. We use this oil to make gasoline. Gas is used to power our cars, heat our homes, and other things. Oil can be expensive, and the countries that have it are often unstable. This is one reason why the price of gas can be so high here in America. Imagine if, instead, we could simply use a gust of wind. That would change the world, don't you think?

Picture a windmill. As the wind blows, the blades on the windmill turn. This is a way of creating electricity. This makes more sense than using machines that require oil to work. If everybody did this, think about how much better it would be for our environment.

People like Sam Salwei and Jason Magness—and Jerry—care about our environment. They have combined this positive attitude with an awesome new sport like snowkiting. Jerry plans to get even more involved with snowkiting. So, if you're ever in North Dakota, look out! You might see a 5-foot-6-inch Asian guy attached to a snowkite with a big grin on his face. Take a close look—it might be Jerry!

**We *did* say snowkiting takes place on the snow. But Jerry likes to do things his own way!**

# Chapter Six

## The Skateboarding
## Vegetarian Pacifist

It was June, the first day of summer vacation. The sun was shining and there was nothing to do all day but skate. What more could Jerry possibly ask for? He grabbed a granola bar, slammed the back door behind him, and jumped on his skateboard. He didn't want to waste one second of summer.

Within moments, Jerry was in a world of his own. First, he spent a couple of minutes skating right out in front of his house. He likes to spread slippery skate wax all over the curb, which makes it really slick. This makes it easy for him and his friends to grind on it. They have spent many afternoons skating there. They do nose grinds, tail slides, board slides, and any other tricks they can land.

When it comes to skateboarding, Jerry has always built clever things. Years ago, he would build rails and boxes to skate on. "It's really not that complicated," he says. "I would take two pieces of PVC pipe and screw them on to a 2 x 4 slab of wood." This created a flat bar, or a long railing. It was cool because the PVC is slick, so it slides perfectly. A skater can grind on it or do his slides.

After landing a few tricks, Jerry headed out. He didn't notice the sounds of dogs barking, birds chirping, or even car horns honking. The headphones of his MP3 player were stuck in his ears. A song called "The Sky," by the indie band The Junior Varsity, blasted through his brain. The thumping of the bass matched the herky-jerky moves Jerry was making on his skateboard.

It was awesome. Cruising down the street, Jerry was popping Ollies and jumping over every little gap he could find. Looking up, he couldn't help but smile. When Jerry is outside on his skateboard, life is good and nothing else matters.

With a grin, Jerry noticed a manhole in the middle of the street. Naturally, he busted an Ollie over it. Skaters are always watching their surroundings with a sharp eye. Everything is fair game, and nothing is off limits. They look for an opportunity to do a Kickflip, a Backside 180 Ollie, or anything else.

The song "Sharks in your Mouth" by the group

I Killed the Prom Queen came on. Jerry turned up the volume. He was pumped, really getting into the music. He was looking to land an even better trick. There was a bus bench at the end of the street. Jerry Ollied up on the front of the bench. He landed on the back two wheels of his board while rolling at high speed. It was like a kicked-up wheelie. Jerry landed perfectly on all four wheels after twisting off the other side of the bench. An Ollie Manual, skillfully performed.

By the time Jerry reached Rocky's house, he was feeling great. It had been an awesome ride and a perfect start to a long summer. While waiting for Rocky to come outside, Jerry eyed the curb. It was painted red. The paint makes the curb a little slippery, so Jerry grinded on it. When Rocky came outside, the two friends were ready to get the party started. They had fun plans for the rest of the day—and for the rest of the summer: a lot of skateboarding.

Jerry is a laid-back skateboarder who has his own way of doing things. Still, it's not like he's a slacker. It would be a mistake to think that he doesn't care about his future. Jerry has always been interested in learning. It's fortunate that he's had several excellent teachers throughout his life. These teachers have given him motivation to work hard.

Jerry has kept up a 3.2 GPA (Grade Point Average). It's a great achievement when you consider the tough classes he's taken throughout high school. Jerry's schedule has always been packed with AP (Advanced Placement) classes. He will already have 23 college credits by the time he starts college!

The next stop for Jerry will be Minnesota State University Moorhead. It's a couple of hours away from Beulah. Like all freshmen, Jerry is looking forward to the experience of living on his own. Without a doubt, he's going to have a busy college career. That's because he's planning to study both math and physics.

Jerry is thinking about becoming a researcher, or maybe even a dentist. Of course, he won't forget about his favorite hobby. "Wherever I work, I'm going to show up with my board. I may even skate to work, during lunch, and then skate back home. It's part of who I am, so I expect it to be with me forever."

Jerry takes on many different roles in his life. He's a great student who can often be seen reading a complicated book. But he doesn't forget to have fun.

He spends a lot of time playing music, skating, snowboarding, snowkiting, and hanging out with his friends. Jerry cannot be easily defined. Just when you think you understand him, he turns things around and surprises you.

One thing that *does* remain consistent is Jerry's creativity. Jerry always finds the time for cool things like music and art. Check out another of his most recent drawings, which he describes as "very emo":

These drawings are a perfect reminder that Jerry is his own guy. That's why he makes decisions based on what he likes. When everybody else is buying an iPod, he shows up with a different MP3 player. When everybody dresses one way, he seems to wear a completely different style.

Jerry's outside-the-box attitude has led him in some interesting directions. That's why he's become a vegetarian and a believer in animal rights. Some people don't eat meat because of health issues. Jerry doesn't eat meat because he doesn't believe in killing animals or using them for food. He understands that many people believe that fish and wildlife are part of a complex food chain. He doesn't have a problem with this point of view. However, he personally doesn't think humans *need* to eat animals. "Being at the top of the food chain, we should be able to find other ways to eat—such as being vegetarians," says Jerry.

Jerry understands that most people eat meat. If you're his friend, he won't give you a hard time about eating a burger. Still, Jerry feels strongly about the cruelty of raising animals for food. He is also worried about the possible health problems. "People should know about the stuff that is pumped into chickens and other animals," Jerry declares. "I don't know about you, but I have serious questions about eating a genetically altered piece of meat."

**Jerry makes his own pizza ... sure beats a geneti-cally altered chicken sandwhich, doesn't it?**

It says a lot about Jerry that he would take this position. Remember, he lives in North Dakota. This is a state where vegetarians are about as common as UFOs. In addition, hunting and fishing are among the most popular local sports. These are activities Jerry would never participate in. He is what's called a pacifist. This means he's against all violence, from animal cruelty to war. He has read a great deal about America's involvement in the Middle East. It's not uncommon to find him discussing the subject with friends.

Jerry will be the first one to tell you that the Middle East is a complicated issue. The area has had problems for centuries. We hear about countries like Iraq, Iran, Israel, Lebanon, Syria, and Saudi Arabia. Sometimes we don't quite understand what it has to do with us here in America.

The United States depends on oil. Remember, it's used to power our cars, farm equipment, and other things. We buy most of this oil from Middle East countries such as Saudi Arabia. Unfortunately, countries in this part of the world have a history of fighting. This affects the world in many ways. When these countries fight, the amount of available oil shrinks. More importantly, people lose their lives in the battles that take place. Many countries have tried to bring peace to the area.

Jerry understands how difficult these conflicts are. Still, as a pacifist, he believes that the United States should stay out of it. He feels that the countries should try to work it out themselves. The cool thing about Jerry is that he's always willing to think about other opinions. He'll never simply try to convince you that he is right and you are wrong.

Unique souls like Jerry will be leading our country in the years to come. That's a good thing. People like Jerry might succeed in bringing about peace to the Middle East—and to the world.

# Chapter Seven

## Twists and Turns

Life has more ups, downs, twists, and turns than a roller coaster. Things happen all the time that completely change the course of life. Sometimes families have to move, forcing kids to start over at new schools. Other times, a death or divorce in the family causes everything to change. Nobody can deny that there's a lot of luck involved in the way life works out. Some people call it fate.

One child is born in a Third World country, while another child is born into English royalty. Not very fair, is it? But that's just the way it is.

Sometimes an accidental event can change the entire course of history. In a weird world, things like this happen. Of course, someone like Austin Gollaher wouldn't call it weird. He would probably just call it fate. Did Mr. Gollaher, who died more than one hundred years ago, actually change history? Incredibly, many people believe so.

Who was Austin Gollaher? Well, he was just a normal 10-year-old boy back in the year 1816. Austin's best friend was a 7-year-old boy named Abe. One day they were hanging out together, looking for stuff to do. They came upon a stream known as "Knob Creek," which was deep and overflowing. The boys wanted to cross the stream. But the only way to walk across was over a narrow log. It was dangerous and a stupid idea, but the boys decided to go for it.

Austin went first and made it across with no problem. Abe, however, slipped and fell into the dangerous, rushing stream. The current was very powerful. Abe wasn't strong enough to make it to the other side. He began to go under. He would have drowned if his friend hadn't been a quick thinker. Austin found a long stick and held it out so that Abe could grab it. Pulling his buddy to shore, Austin shook him and rolled him around on the ground. Water poured out of Abe's mouth and nose. If not for Austin, Abe would have died that day.

Good thing he didn't. Abe was short for Abraham—as in Abraham Lincoln. The little kid who nearly drowned ended up becoming the 16th president of the United States. Austin Gollaher saved one of the most important figures in American history.

The Lincoln Memorial, in Washington D.C., honors Abraham Lincoln.

Here's another example: A baby boy is born in a foreign country. A twist of fate brings him to the United States. That baby grows up into a teenager with an awesome future ahead of him. His name: Darren Craig Schaeffer, aka Jerry.

Jerry is originally from South Korea. He was put up for adoption soon after being born in 1989. Luckily, Mr. and Mrs. Schaeffer came along. They had decided to adopt a baby from a foreign country.

In order to adopt a baby, the Schaeffers learned all about South Korea. It was only fair that they respect the country in which Jerry was born. Jerry doesn't remember any of this, of course. However, he does have some memories from three years later. He and his parents went back to South Korea to adopt another baby. That little girl became his kid sister, Jamie.

**The South Korean flag . . . from the country of Jerry and Jamie's birth.**

Things have worked out very well for Jerry and Jamie. And they are not alone. Many people might be surprised to hear how many adoptions take place in the United States. The numbers are pretty amazing. Over the last 20 years there have been more than 100,000 adoptions per year. Most of them involve American children, but not all.

Foreign adoption has received a great deal of attention over the last several years. This is mainly because of the celebrities who have gotten involved. It made international headlines when Madonna adopted a baby from Malawi in 2006. Brad Pitt and Angelina Jolie have also adopted children from different countries.

Jerry certainly isn't in awe of people like Brad Pitt or Madonna. He does respect them for what they have done, though. He knows that growing up in the United States has advantages. He never would have had the same opportunities in South Korea. He plans to make the most of them.

Many people who were adopted have gone on to lead successful lives. Some of them have even found fame and fortune. Have you ever eaten at Wendy's? Dave Thomas, the owner, was adopted when he was only six weeks old. From the time he was young, he always dreamed of owning a hamburger restaurant. Maybe that dream wouldn't have come true if a loving family hadn't taken him into their home.

**You won't catch Jerry eating one of these, but things sure worked out for Dave Thomas!**

You've surely heard of Apple, as in the company that makes and sells iPods, iPhones, and Mac computers. Apple is one of the most successful companies in America. Many years ago, a couple in California named Paul and Clara Jobs decided to adopt a child. That baby was Steve Jobs, who would later become the co-founder of Apple.

Is any of this fate? Coincidence? Nobody knows for sure. Let's face it, in many ways this is a weird world. Exciting, beautiful, and colorful, but weird—and that's what makes it interesting. Everybody loves ice cream. But how dull would it be if the only two flavors were chocolate and vanilla? It's the same way with people. Throughout history, there have been unique souls changing the world for the better. They were creative, original, and ahead of their time. In many cases, they were laughed at or thought of as crazy.

Anyone who has ever taken American History in school has read about Christopher Columbus. This explorer set sail in 1492. He wasn't scared or put off by rumors of "boiling water," or "sea monsters." Some people thought that sailing out into the Atlantic Ocean was insane. Still, Columbus followed his heart. He wasn't the kind of person who accepted popular ideas. This type of spirit led to the discovery of the new world.

Columbus is just one example. There are thousands more. You can look at almost any period in history. You will find people who changed medicine, politics, sports, and almost every other field. Here's an example that can't even be credited to any one particular individual...

New York, mid 1970s . . . young people in the inner city are unhappy with the music they hear on the radio. Street DJs begin using turntables to play their favorite drum sounds in exciting patterns. Eventually, they begin speaking over the beat. The idea is to get people hyped, and encourage audience participation.

This was the beginning of what would come to be known as hip hop. In the early days, DJs were criticized for creating this new type of music. As a matter of fact, most critics wouldn't even admit it was music. They figured it wouldn't last. How very wrong they were!

As this modern style of music began to gain momentum, more people joined in. Everyone wanted to get up to take their turn on the microphone. They started "rapping" over the steady beat of drums or instrumental tracks. This quickly caught on and developed. The sounds became more complex, adding "samples" of other songs.

The Sugarhill Gang released the song "Rapper's Delight" in 1979. With that song, rap music officially exploded onto the music scene. It's now as big a part of popular culture as any other type of music.

Individuals with originality and imagination keep at it—just like Christopher Columbus, Picasso, the Wright brothers, and the creators of rap music. The world owes a lot to these unique souls. We celebrate them and wait for the next generation of creators. They are among us, there's no doubt about it. These bold people take time to consider the world around them.

They don't blindly follow the crowd. Maybe *you* are one of them. After all, we are all very creative in our own way. None of us should be afraid to follow our dreams. We are each an important piece in the complicated puzzle of this weird world.

How does Jerry fit into this complicated puzzle? He's not sure—which is exactly the way it should be at this point in his life. His journey is like a bumpy, thrilling, downhill ride on a skateboard. It's not clear where his journey will take him. With his creative mind and enthusiasm for life, he has plenty in store for the world. It's obvious that the world has many cool things in store for him as well.

Darren "Jerry" Schaeffer—a unique soul, living in a weird world.

**Be you.**